Saturday Morning

And Other Stories

Michael G. Bausch

"Saturday Morning" was first published in *Century 1969*, The Carroll College Magazine of the Creative Arts, 1969.

"The Spirit of Geneva Lake" appeared in *Lake Geneva Magazine*, Volume 1, Issue 4, August 1988.

"Owl, Ice, and I" was published by the Amherst Society in the *1988 American Poetry Annual.*

Cover Photo:

The author is seated on the lap of his grandfather Armand C. Weiss and across from his grandfather Jacob P. Bausch and is being introduced to the joys of coffee at a very young age.

ISBN: 978-0-9864407-1-7
ISBN-13: 9780986440717

CONTENTS

INTRODUCTION 1

SATURDAY MORNING...6

19 HOURS IN MEMPHIS 10

LESSONS FROM THE WEIGHT ROOM.......................38

WHAT WOULD JESUS DRIVE? 43

ARNIE..46

SMOKY LINK..48

THE SPIRIT OF GENEVA LAKE.....................................60

OWL, ICE, AND I...64

LA BELLE CEMETERY 65

WHEN A FAMILY PET DIES...72

INTRODUCTION

In the winter and spring of 2017 I thought it time to start cleaning out some of my old files and review what I've written – and saved – over the years. There was some good material, and in some cases only the original printed copy, which meant a few of my older writings were not in a retrievable computer file I could simply upload and edit. "Saturday Morning," for example, was preserved in the original magazine in which the story was published and a carbon copy of a typewritten version.

My only copy of "19 Hours in Memphis" was printed on an old dot-matrix computer printer, with the original computer file on which it was created and stored (on a 5" floppy disk for an old CP/M computer) now gone.

With the magic of today's technology, I was able to convert these documents into new formats by scanning them into digital files, and with OCR (optical character recognition) tools turn them into Google Docs and Word documents. This process took some time, but was pleasurable in and of itself.

Once scanned and converted, I started editing these stories word by word. In most cases I wanted to keep the original versions of the story, and in other cases I needed to clean them up a bit. One exception was "Saturday Morning," my first published story because I wanted to preserve this youthful bit of writing.

What follows is a brief explanation of each of the stories contained in this little book. Each one is based on personal experience, although, as you shall see, "Smoky Link" is a fictional account of something I was told had actually happened.

Saturday Morning

When I was a student at Carroll College (the one in Waukesha, Wisconsin) I took a January term course in writing. After a number of writing exercises, my professor asked if she could publish my short essay "Saturday Morning" in a college publication. This is my first published story, and in it I tell the story of a Saturday morning coffee break with my grandfather. I wrote it from the perspective of me as a youngster. The story was published in *Century 1969*, The Carroll College Magazine of the Creative Arts. The grandfather featured in the story is Jacob P. Bausch, the one seated on the right in the cover photo.

19 Hours In Memphis

I've always liked to take occasional short solo travel adventures, and this story tells the tale of a trip from a small town in Wisconsin to the big town of Memphis, Tennessee, where I went to see an exhibit about the treasures of Pharaoh Ramses II of Memphis, Egypt. Being all alone in a new city can be a challenge, and this story is partly about how meeting other people can make the unfamiliar more familiar. Traveling to the American south as a white northerner, I would also encounter an interesting diversity of black/African-American culture and experience.

Lessons From The Weight Room

Never having any interest in bodybuilding or lifting a single weight, I found myself deciding at the age of 40 that I should do something to improve my volleyball game. This story offers my observations from the weight room.

What Would Jesus Drive?

While driving behind a car with the bumper sticker "What Would Jesus Do" (WWJD), I wondered "What Would Jesus *Drive*"?

Arnie

While serving a church located on Geneva Lake, Wisconsin, I was asked to do a number of "lake weddings" on a large tourist boat. During these weddings I'd cruise for four hours with 150 people I didn't know, my only acquaintances being the bride and groom. This gave me the opportunity to strike up conversations with new people, and Arnie was one of them.

Smoky Link

My first summer job between high school and college was working in a meat-packing plant. My job was mainly trimming fat off meat, trimming the meat off the bones, and then grinding and packing hamburger. There was a slaughterhouse next to our facility, and one afternoon, when they were desperate for extra help, my boss asked me to fill in during the hog kill. My experiences that day helped me write a fictional account of the true story I was told of the time a hog got free, ran out of the slaughterhouse, and jumped into the river to swim across to freedom.

The Spirit of Geneva Lake

Living near this lake, I was able to experience the four

seasons on the lake and reflect on the unique relationship that the lake offered. Particularly memorable experiences including skiing on the lake in a snowstorm and ice skating beneath the stars on a cold and clear winter's night. A poem I wrote about the skating was included with my essay that was published in *Lake Geneva Magazine* in 1988.

Owl, Ice, and I

This is the poem I mentioned in *The Spirit of Geneva Lake*. It was published by the Amherst Society in the *1988 American Poetry Annual*.

La Belle Cemetery

In the early 1900s my great-grandfather was a chauffeur for a wealthy family from St. Louis. That family would bring the servants (and their families) from their household on a train to Oconomowoc, Wisconsin, where they'd all spend the summer. My great-grandparents would later return to Wisconsin to make it home, and both would be buried in La Belle Cemetery. Oconomowoc would become a place where their daughter, my grandmother, and her husband, my grandfather, would visit friends and go fishing on Lac La Belle. I fished that lake many times with my grandfather and a friend of his, and once he took grandma and me to the cemetery on the adjacent Fowler Lake to visit the graves of grandma's parents. This account is from a visit some 25 years later.

When A Family Pet Dies

My first experience with the death of a pet was also my two daughters' first experience, and when it was all over I thought I'd report our experience as a way to help others with children when they'd have to go through something similar. I asked a few friends who were small-animal veterinarians to read this, and they thought it good enough to make into a brochure for their offices, but I never went ahead with that project. I wrote the story in 1989 and copyrighted it through my company, The BlueWater Press. This was my only story for that company.

Thank you for your interest in these stories. I hope you enjoy reading them. Maybe they'll inspire you to pay attention to details of the adventures in your own life and enjoy them again by writing them down and one day sharing them with others.

Michael Bausch
August 2017

SATURDAY MORNING

It's Saturday morning. The sun is peeking through the trees, and the leaves slowly rustle in the warm spring breeze. I hear the different sounds of the birds: the robins, the blue jays, the blackbirds, the sparrows, all engaging in their early-morning chatter. I see a robin washing himself in the birdbath. A squirrel comes and scares the robin away and picks out one of the choice pieces of hard, stale bread from those I threw out several minutes before.

The flower garden is beginning to bloom; the lilacs burst with colors of green, white, blue, and blue-gray, and the snap dragons with their velvet insides sway in the breeze. The grass is green and thick, and I can see the dew on the blades. The view from the screened porch is beautiful, and I can smell and feel the warm, sensuous breezes and hear the air broken only by the flitting chirps of the birds.

I move inside to the kitchen, and Grandma tells me to get Grandpa. Bursting with the anticipatory excitement I always get when 10 a.m. rolls around, I run out the kitchen onto the porch, open the door with a click, and run into the grass as the door slams and the screens make their little noises that collectively make a twang. I pass over the old sidewalk where the concrete is textured in small pencil eraser-size stones that create a rough feeling when scraped.

Grandpa is on the side of the lawn in one of his flower beds. "Grandpa, it's time for our coffee break." Without even looking up Grandpa continues to rustle the black earth with his gloved fingers and pull the weeds from the broken-up ground. He stands up with a handful of stringy roots and small ovals of dirt, shakes the matter, and throws the remaining roots into his bushel basket. At the same time he chuckles and says, "Already!" and grins at me with his nice, happy, "it's a beautiful day" face. "Does Grandma have the water ready?" he asks, and I reply, "Yes, come on" in my pleading sort of way. He picks up his basket of weeds, walks behind the garage to what he calls the mulch bed, and dumps the weeds into the wooden box where we dig for worms every time we go fishing.

He continues on his easy way, putting the basket into the garage, taking off his gloves, and putting them on the cluttered workbench. He looks at his African violet sitting in a vase, which is surrounded by envelopes of all types of seeds – small ones, big ones, white ones, black ones, thread-like brittle ones, and round, hard ones.

He stops and straightens the fishnet hanging on the nail in the wall, taking his time. I can't stand it. I want to get into the house where Grandma has the white mugs at our places and the cookies in a dish in the middle of the table, but I know I've still got to wait for Grandpa to get ready for his coffee break.

We walk out of the dark, cool garage into the warm sunlight and the breeze-filled, bird-filled, flower-filled air and slowly make our way to the porch. There, looming right in front of our feet, is a small, green weed on the sidewalk. Grandpa stoops down and picks up the weed, and I say, "I'll throw it into the worm box (I didn't like the big word mulch), and you go get ready."

The door opens – click, clack – and shuts – click, clack. The feet stomp once, twice on the rug, and they slowly walk on the hollow-sounding floor. I hurry from the worm box, open the door – click – and let it go – slam! – and the screen twangs as I patter into the house and see no Grandpa at the table but hear the water in the bathroom going. He's washing his hands, and I go to watch him as he gets the dirt from under his nails, scrubs each portion of his hands, and rolls the right hand in the left in his own special way in an infinitely graceful and slick movement.

Now it's my turn, and I try to roll my small hands as he did with his big ones, but I can't copy his movement. I hurry because he's already in the dining room, looking at the violets, lifting the leaves, bending down, studying the plant, and now moving to get his watering pot with the long spout the thickness of a pencil. He puts some water from the kitchen tap into the can and waters a few violets.

At last he sets the can back under the sink where he got it and sits down at the table, where Grandma has two white mugs on saucers, two spoons, and a plate of big, hard oatmeal cookies. She puts some instant coffee into Grandpa's cup, pours in the boiling water, stirs it, and gives it to him. She gets the red-and-white Sealtest carton containing the milk and pours it into the green pitcher on the table.

Grandpa turns the handle towards him and pours a stream of white milk into the black coffee and stirs it with his spoon in his own way. He takes a drink and looks outside his window and sees his backyard. Meanwhile, Grandma gives me some water, and I stir my coffee and see its wispy steam and smell its richness. Grandpa pours some milk so I have a whole half a cup of coffee and says, "How about a cookie, hmm, Michael?"

He takes one from the dish. I grab one, and we both start to dunk. Grandma sits down at the end of the small table where Grandpa and I sit opposite each other, and she asks him a question about the next-door neighbors. But I don't listen. I'm too busy dunking that cookie into my coffee, a teeny bit until it's soaked, losing a crumb or two in the process, and then eat the moist, soggy portion. The greatest mouth-watering taste to try to describe is the taste of dunked cookie. Pretty soon I've dunked so much all I have is a cup full of mushy crumbs, and I don't want to drink that.

So, I climb up on Grandpa's lap and dunk a cookie into his coffee. He holds me firmly and hugs me and says, "Are you getting bigger?" I say, "Yup!" We both look out the window at the bird flopping in the birdbath, the blackbirds eating the hard bread left over from the squirrel, and the lilacs blooming. We also see the snapdragons and green grass, smell the fresh, spring air, and share the sunlight on the backyard as the sun slowly makes its way up the sky.

Saturday morning is ending.

19 HOURS IN MEMPHIS

I've found that taking a personal "adventure trip" every now and then is a great way to get a fresh view on life. In the spring of 1987, I decided to take a trip to Memphis, Tennessee.

I'd read about an exhibit of Egyptian artifacts from the period of Ramses II, possibly the biblical Pharaoh of the Hebrew Exodus, in five cities of the United States, and decided I'd like to go to that. I received information from the Denver Museum, but found the timing would be better for me to go to the Memphis exhibit. I found out that Amtrak offered a $118 round trip fare, so I decided to go.

I phoned the Memphis Ticketron and got a ticket for a 1 p.m. viewing of the exhibit on Tuesday, April 21. I then worked on Amtrak reservations. Scheduling was no problem because there were no choices. The "City of New Orleans" left Union Station in Chicago at 6:45 p.m. and arrived in Memphis at 5:10 a.m. The return trip would leave Memphis at 11:59 p.m. and arrive back in Chicago at 11:50 a.m. I decided to leave Monday night, April 20 and return at 11:59 the next night. I would spend eighteen hours in Memphis.

Making the train reservations proved to be a little more challenging than I figured. Only a certain number of seats were available at the reduced fare, which by then had fallen to $92. There was a seat available coming back, but not leaving on the day I wanted. I was told to call after midnight, when the reservations that had not been confirmed by ticket purchase would be cancelled by the computer. After a midnight call, I was told to call at 3 a.m. when indeed the reservations would have been cleared. So I set the alarm, went to sleep a couple hours, awoke at 3 a.m., and then confirmed my reservations. My journey had begun – it was a trip just to get a train reservation!

Riding The Rails

The day came. I drove my "whisper jet" '77 Honda Accord 30 minutes to the Fox Lake, Illinois, train station, parked the car, and got on the 3:10 train to Union Station in Chicago. A couple of older women got in my car and started partying with their Seagram's peach wine coolers. Their party reflected the weather: it was a sunny, clear, and warm day. I traveled light, bringing only a small backpack with yogurt, carrots, and cheese for supper; some notebooks, books, and pens; and a change of underwear.

Arriving in Chicago, I strolled Union Station and did some people-watching. It wasn't long before I could board the train, and soon we began to roll at 6:51 p.m. On my car were twenty-five others, all black, journeying to Memphis. Other cars had white students and professor types heading to Champaign and Carbondale, Illinois, university towns. I traveled with the salt of the earth.

The train ride was a real pleasure. I love that ride through south Chicago, where you see the different layers of Chicago life: abandoned factories, row houses, backyards, dilapidated buildings, deserted streets, then residential areas with people (blacks) sitting on porches and stoops or playing games in the streets. I noticed a sign stretched across a street that was flanked by beat-up buildings, litter, and general disrepair: "Welcome to Kensington, the Pearl of Southern Chicago."

After a while we moved through the white areas where the houses are farther apart, the trees and bushes are everywhere, and people are nowhere to be seen. Riding the train through these areas is like going through the backyard of all these communities – and a sensory delight.

I watched the sun set as a red ball in the west and thought about California a moment as I saw two lines of clouds running through the sun. I thought about the train ride and how much better it is to travel by car or bus or train than by airplane. You have a better sense of time, and you experience the scenery and the fatigue. I'd like to walk someday and experience that sense of journeying, to go thirty miles with a group of folks, taking our sleeping bags and a Bible and acting as if we lived 2,000 years ago. We'd talk about our lives and about biblical stories, find food however we could, sleep in a church somewhere, and experience a "community of the walk." A peripatetic community.

This journey brings the "spiritual journey" metaphor to life: The destination is not the important thing, but the journey itself presents excitement and many possibilities for meaning and learning. The way, the process, the "between the no longer and the not yet" are ways of speaking of living in the present moment with little thought for the future. I remember reading somewhere about looking at one's life as if it were a train journey. If you knew the destination was your death, wouldn't you treasure the journey a bit more? Once you arrived, it was all over. Too many of us are not happy until we "get there" and forget that we are already "there," wherever we are, and that the journey itself can be the destination.

I love these short trips. They allow me thoughts like this. They allow me time to reflect, to see different scenery, to be reminded I am part of a larger human race and a larger human landscape. I think that here I am, traveling 24 hours, the only sleep to be on a train seat, in order to spend another 18 hours in a strange city, with the main objective being to see an exhibit of ancient artifacts! If all I wanted was to get to my destination and see old museum objects, I wouldn't spend the time or the effort! Obviously the journey itself is a major reason for the trip.

Given my anticipated 5 a.m. arrival, I thought it best to forego the lounge car and get some rest. I watched out the window, read, wrote, and decided to sleep at 10 p.m. No one sat with me, so I could "stretch" out on the seat, and managed to sleep in three or four basic positions. I did get thirsty at one point and went to the bathroom, where I talked with a couple black men heading to Mississippi. It was basic late-night urinal chatter. The woozy kind when everyone is tired. It was friendly.

During the night there were several stops, and at one point the train completely shut down – no ventilation, no lights, not a sound, save for the murmurs and rustles of my sleeping-car companions. It was as if we were all together in a great dormitory, strangers to one another, yet trusting ourselves to each other in sleep. We were stopped like that for about twenty minutes, and I later found out this was a routine stop for a switching procedure.

Arrival

We arrived in Memphis at 6 a.m., fifty minutes late, but I really didn't mind. Dawn was starting to break, it was warm, and I was ready. I planned to walk from the station to downtown, which by my map was about two miles north. I was surprised by the train "station" being a small room with a couple of rows of chairs, but my big surprise

13

was yet to come.

I stepped outside and found I was in what appeared to be a war zone. Everywhere I looked I saw unpainted brick buildings, most with windows and doors boarded up. I saw a bus go by, so I figured there was life, but I was spooked as I walked up Main Street, the only human on the streets, passing billiard halls that were closed just a few hours before and watching doorways for anything suspicious. I was a Williams Bay boy and had lost my San Francisco Tenderloin street smarts and ease, and was a mite fearful. I wondered how long I could walk these dead streets as a lone human being, a white country boy in what seemed to be a war zone.

In the next block I was surprised to see a new firehouse and felt instant comfort knowing there were other humans around and possibly a source of some directions. As I crossed the street I spotted a sign that froze my gaze: "Lorraine Motel."

I walked the half block to the sign and the chills of historic recognition swept over me: There were the familiar-looking pink doors and yellow-trimmed walls bounded by a black metal railing. And then I saw it, the room from which Dr. Martin Luther King had emerged before he was shot on the balcony. The room's door had a large wreath upon it, and now protecting the doorway out to the railing itself (too late, I'd say) was a plastic enclosure with another wreath upon it. Next to the room are a suite for a black history group and a poverty group's office.

The motel is still a place for folks to stay, and I could tell that by the disheveled curtains in several windows. A few old cars seemed to litter the parking lot, and a lone gray cat stood and watched me.

A large car cruised by, and then a van, and someone was walking along a street, and I remembered that I wasn't comfortable in this neighborhood. I returned to the fire station and found a bench under a tree, and decided to take stock of where I was, where I was going, and how I was going to get there.

After a few minutes of appreciating the fact that I was OK and that I could handle this quite well, I got up and continued my walk north up the deserted streets. After three blocks of boarded windows and doors, and no signs of life, I heard a bus, and I decided to stand at the bus stop. I got on realizing I didn't have change, but was happy to see the machine took dollar bills. After I inserted my dollar for the $.85 fare, I stood rather dumbly watching the machine to see what would happen as if this were some kind of slot machine, and the driver calmly said, "It don't make change."

I turned around to find a seat and realized I was the only white on this bus, and everyone seemed to be looking at me and my light blue pants and white shirt and tennis shoes and blue backpack, saying, "How in the world did he get here?"

But at last I felt comfortable, with other people, going north to downtown Memphis. I got off near two huge churches, one Presbyterian and the other Methodist, and walked toward the Civic Center, where I would be returning at 1 p.m. There were a few people around, mostly white government office workers, and they were coming to work.

For the most part, I was the only person around. I

walked the Mid-America Mall, which is downtown Memphis' attempt at restoration. I noticed how some stores had simply closed up already and were relocated at suburban sites. There were too many stores with windows boarded up.

I still felt a bit strange, with few people around. It was only 6:30 in the morning and most workers wouldn't be coming until at least 8 a.m. I walked by Confederate Park on a bluff overlooking the Mississippi and read a few of the historical markers. It seems the Confederates held the bluff when Union forces attacked from the river but eventually lost the entire city. There were a few street types sitting on benches, and I didn't feel like making conversation.

I returned to the Mid-America Mall, bought some orange juice in a drugstore that just opened, and then went to sit in a lovely park filled with squirrels and pigeons and a few street people. The morning sun was getting hot, and I could tell it was going to be a scorcher.

One of the guys sitting about fifty yards away, a black guy in tattered clothes walked by me, and I looked at him and said, "Mornin'." He looked at me and he said, "Who is you, man?" And I rather cheerfully replied, "My name is Mike." And he kind of looked and kept on walking.

I began to feel like a total fool. He obviously didn't want to know my name. Was he using an updated 1987 version of the old 1970s greeting, "What it is, man"? Or was he seeing a stranger to his part of the world and wondering whom it was who was intruding on his turf? I started feeling like a real farm boy in the big city! And I continued to feel a bit strange about my relationship to this southern city.

The young white professionals began to be more apparent, the legal eagles and county and federal bureaucrats. The only people who sat were young and poor.

The Peabody Hotel

One of the places I wanted to see was the Peabody. In Memphis they say "PEE-body." Now I know in Boston they say "pee-b-dy." I went to the Peabody because I had read in the *Smithsonian* or *National Geographic* about the Peabody ducks. There are trained ducks at the hotel who make a grand entrance each day, and I figured I might as well see that.

The hotel is a real beauty, restored from a bygone era. The lobby is exquisite with a large marble fountain as the centerpiece and a bar nearby. There are sofas, tables, and chairs nicely arranged in the lobby and a large piano nearby. There seemed to be many high school kids around, and there were dozens of well-dressed and beautiful women about. It turned out there was a secretaries convention at the hotel. The scenery, and feel of the city, was greatly improving.

I walked up some stairs and looked into a main ballroom, complete with chandeliers, pillars, a stage, and ornate ceiling work. I saw a piano that was once owned by Francis Scott Key and looked at the Peabody Memorabilia Room, filled with letters from famous visitors such as Harry Truman (the only name I knew).

I found a bathroom and decided to freshen up a bit and put on a tie (so I'd look as if I belonged to the Peabody). A guy in a gray pinstripe three-piece suit walked in to take a leak, and he looked at me and my backpack like "what boat did you just get off of," but I let him take a leak and didn't bother him any. Though I guess I must have bothered him because he forgot to wash his hands.

Going back downstairs I checked out the menu in the Peabody restaurant, and thought I might come back for an expensive dinner. I figured I deserved it after the morning I'd been having.

Then I walked over to the concierge desk to look at some literature and see how much it cost to go see Graceland. Not that I really wanted to do that, but if I had some time, and it wasn't too expensive, I could always pay my respects. But then I found out that the ducks made their entrance at 11 a.m., and since I had to be at the museum by 1 p.m., I figured there wasn't time for Elvis. Besides, it would have been very expensive, and I would have had to take one of those Gray Line tours with the other tourists. And I didn't even bring my camera!

The concierge was very friendly and dignified in his gray morning coat. After we had talked a while, he gave me many hints on where to go and what to see and told me how wonderful the Ramses II exhibit was. He spoke with many of the beautiful women, which made my conversation with him highly pleasurable. After he gave me a better map of downtown, I plotted my 9:30-10:30 a.m. strategy.

Front Street

I walked outside, felt the heat, and noticed one bank thermometer that read 92 degrees! It was going to be a scorcher. By now there were many people on the streets of Memphis, and I walked west toward the Mississippi. I strolled along some riverfront restaurants and watched trucks being unloaded for the day's menus.

I saw a kiosk with photos of the old days of cotton, with people driving their wagons to this area for loading and unloading onto the riverboats. I turned the corner, heading east again, and wound up on Front Street. The buildings were old, some brick, some wood, and most had signs such as J. Flake & Co. with words identifying the buildings as cotton companies.

I walked into one, and the room was warm, long, and narrow. As far as I could see there were tables full of cotton. A young black man walked in and sat at a dingy desk, and I asked him where this cotton came from. He said from the "me-ill," which after some thought meant "mill" to a northerner. I told him I felt sorry for him that he had to sit inside that hot room on such a day as this, and he readily accepted my pity.

Outside again, I walked some more on the red brick sidewalk and passed huge bales of cotton sitting on the sidewalk. Old black men hauled the stuff in and out of buildings, while white manager types came and went at will; it seemed as if I was back in the 19th century. I stopped at a corner cafe for a 10 a.m. hot dog and chocolate milk, which became both breakfast and lunch. I sat at a table outdoors and turned so I could see the cotton on the sidewalks and marvel at the sense of time warp. Next to me was Carter's seed store, and elderly black women were there buying tomato starts, peanuts, and hanging plants, possibly as the women had done for decades.

The Duck March

After the hot dog on Front Street, I felt ready for the ducks at the Peabody. I entered the lobby and pulled up a chair. Many tables were full of people, and a cocktail waitress was coming around for drink orders. Several tables were full of elderly white ladies who had arrived early for a good seat and to sip their coffee. It must be a daily ritual for some. Young tourist types or folks on convention were drinking bloody marys and Irish coffee.

A preschool class gathered in the lobby, and others began to come to fill in available space. All the good seats by the fountain were taken. At 10:50 a porter brought three red-carpeted steps, which he placed in front of the fountain, and then rolled out a red carpet from the fountain to the elevator, a distance of about thirty yards. Children and adults lined the carpet, eagerly awaiting the ducks. Others began to stand, while still others began taking photos of the carpet, fountain, friends, etc.

I recognized an older black gentleman who got on the elevator and went up: I knew he was the ducks' trainer from a photo I had seen. He was going to the Penthouse "Duck Palace" where the ducks lived. They came down at 11 a.m. every day to swim in the fountain for their six-hour shift and then returned to the elevator and their suite at 5 p.m. sharp.

It was getting close to 11 a.m., and the energy level was picking up in the lobby. I watched a businessman, acting nonchalant, join the throng of elderly women, preschoolers, and photographing parents in expectation. I looked above and behind me and noticed one or two people standing on a balcony and decided to go up there to get a view of the whole event.

From the balcony I watched the clock and the elevator. All eyes were on the elevator, the center one of three in the lobby. We watched the light indicate it was coming down, and when the door opened two businessmen got off. No ducks yet.

But then a man stood by the elevator, with microphone in hand, and at the stroke of 11 o'clock announced in a deep voice, "Ladies and gentlemen, the Peabody Hotel welcomes you." The elevator door opened.

Inside I could see two ducks running around. There was a man with them. The crowd stretched and stirred and murmured with excitement. Suddenly, at command, the ducks raced out of the elevator. I expected they would march with dignity, but no, they ran as fast as they could, not in the straight line I expected, but in a wavy pattern.

A mallard led the group of four females, and one by one they jumped up the red-carpeted steps, and hopped into the fountain. Everyone cheered, flashbulbs popped, and the ducks swam in some kind of clockwise, then counterclockwise, movement around the fountain.

They ate some food left on some pedestals in the fountain and swam around. People began to leave, but the best show was developing, as the mallard was horny. The mallard proceeded to hop on each one of the females, providing some parents an embarrassing moment and the rest of us who looked on an amusing show.

The lobby piano began to play, and it took a while before I realized no one was playing it – some kind of computer was operating the keys. The invisible pianist provided music for ducks to screw by in the ornate Peabody lobby.

The Woman On The Balcony

Standing next to me throughout the show was a youngish-looking woman. She was about 5'5" tall, with dark and graying hair, about 43 years old, slender, and wearing strange-looking tinted glasses. Later I noticed she was wearing an official button-down Peabody Hotel striped shirt, with a small duck emblem over the left breast. She was enjoying the show and made a comment about how she loves to come and watch it. We began to chat, and it turned out she was here from New York and she was working on a film about Memphis music. She introduced herself as "Lynn."

She had been interviewing Carl Perkins, Johnny Cash, and some lesser known elderly black talent (lesser known to me, at least). While we watched the mallard hopping on the hens she asked me what brought me to Memphis. I showed her my excellent photo of the huge statue of Ramses from Memphis, and she excitedly remarked that I should write an article about my trip to Memphis, Egypt, and Memphis, Tennessee, with accompanying photos. There would be a market for that, she said, and it would make for an interesting story.

I asked her what I should see while here. Should I go to Beale Street? Should I go anywhere to hear the "Memphis sound?" She advised me not to go to Beale Street as it was a tourist trap and had very little to do with authentic local music. She also warned me about the danger on the streets (that I had already sensed) and suggested I might not want to be on the streets walking to Amtrak that night—it was a dangerous area to move through.

She liked to say "what the hell" and "Christ" a lot as

22

she talked, and there was something about her that said she wasn't real secure. Yet she clearly was an artist devoted to the craft of filmmaking and writing, and I told her I admired her for her commitment and devotion to that craft. It obviously was a driving force in her life, and she was forsaking, I felt, all other attachments for her profession.

She made several negative comments about children and teenagers during our talks and did not seem to be a type of person who sought loving commitments. I kept feeling good about the conversation, and it kept on quite easily. At one point she asked me the fateful question, "What do you do?" Without hesitation I told her I was a minister. She didn't say anything about it, and we didn't bring it up again.

We stood on the balcony and talked for a while. During that time two women came up to her who recognized her from some temporary work she had done with a social agency for a few months to earn some rent money. These women were there for the secretaries convention in the hotel.

The time was approaching when I should begin the hike to the Convention Center and indicated that. She began to walk with me through the Mid-America Mall, and it felt good to have a companion. We chatted as we walked along the mall, watching the many people on lunch hour and the black men in long lines sitting on walls and watching the walkers.

She walked with me all the way to the center. Just as we were approaching it an elderly white man came up to us, said he had an extra ticket to the exhibit, and offered it to her at no cost. She accepted his generous offer, thanked him, and invited him to meet her for a drink across the street at the end of the afternoon.

We entered the hall and went to the cafeteria for something cold to drink. (My actual journal entry ended just before I met her in the Peabody balcony. The events of the rest of the day happened so fast I didn't take time to write them. I write now on the basis of memory one month later.) We talked pleasantly and watched in amazement as hundreds and hundreds of Memphis schoolchildren ended their tour and swarmed over the gift shop. We had to wait in several lines before we could enter the exhibit. 100,000 Memphis kids would see the exhibit before mid-June, and this was creating a logistical problem for the exhibit folks.

Our delay was fifteen or twenty minutes, and soon we were each decked out with a tape cassette of the exhibit narrated by Charlton Heston (I guess because of his "Moses" fame and that connection with Ramses II, possible pharaoh of the Exodus.) and ready to go to the film introduction to the exhibit.

We sat in a room with mainly elderly white folks and watched the three-projector/simultaneous/with-dissolve-program detailing some of Ramses' history. I enjoyed seeing some of the places I had seen in Egypt; Lynn was most impressed with the photography and said it was an excellent presentation. I had seen the same quality in seminary projects 13 years earlier, but didn't mention it to my newly made filmmaker friend.

We began touring the exhibit together and commented to each other about the exquisite work on some of the pieces.

The Exhibit

I should preface these comments by noting that I had seen the Tutankhamen exhibit in San Francisco in 1977, had been to the Egyptian Museum in Cairo in 1984, and had been to Memphis and Luxor/Karnak, Egypt, in 1984. I have seen the best Egypt has to offer, and thus this exhibit was not as spectacular.

Many of the pieces were simply period pieces, readily seen in places like the Oriental Museum in Chicago, or any art museum in this country. Once you've seen one coffin lid, you've pretty much seen them all.

Because Ramses' tomb had been plundered maybe 3,000 years ago, there is very little material from the time of Ramses anyway, and this exhibit was inherently at a disadvantage when compared with that of Tutankhamen.

Perhaps the most striking parts of the exhibit were:

1) an open-air shrine, from a sun sanctuary of Ramses, complete with a "corridor" lined with four baboons, and the shrine itself, about 3' high and 4' at the base, containing a scarab beetle and a baboon, and decorated on the sides with reliefs of Ramses in action. The baboon represented Thoth, the god of scribes and written things, and is important to sun worship because the baboon screams at sunrise, much like our roosters. The beetle has the peculiar habit of rolling its dung in little balls, and the Egyptians figured a giant beetle rolled the sun ball across the sky. The beetles also lay their eggs in dung, so new life emerges from the dung balls and, by extension, from worship of the sun ball. I now know why the Israelites couldn't stand Egyptian religion. Not only did it have a sociopolitical bias towards the rich, but the religion worshiped monkeys and dung-

rolling bugs.

2) the goat vessel, made of gold and silver. The vessel itself was shaped like a pomegranate, with inscriptions and artwork depicting battle and hunting scenes. The handle is a golden goat, with its hind legs at the middle of the vessel, the body stretched up toward the lip, and the goat's mouth biting the lip, thus completing the handle. The tiny eyes of the goat are absolutely intent on biting that lip hard, and the detail the artist rendered is lifelike, down to the hair on the goat's back and the texture of the inner ear.

3) the gold of valor, a 19-pound necklace composed of 5,000 flat gold disk beads strung on heavy thread fastened to a lapis lazuli-inlaid gold plaque. Suspended from this are 14 gold braided chains divided first into two and then into four strands at the bottom of the necklace. This was found on a mummy (not Ramses) and was given in return for bravery or courage.

I took my time as I went through the exhibit; after all, I had traveled a long way, and I wasn't about to walk through this swiftly. I lost Lynn, but continued on, examining each piece in as much detail as I could. When I would see painted coffin lids, or tomb doors, I would get as close as I could to see the brush strokes and feel the living presence of the artist who had once created the piece.

It took me the full two hours to thoroughly enjoy the exhibit. I walked down the stairs, deposited the Heston tape and player, and entered the gift shop. I was on assignment from Cathy to bring home T-shirts and posters. I also looked for a book about Ramses. Two hours earlier Lynn had remarked, "I don't understand why people get T-shirts at these things." She seemed to have a noncommercial streak to her in addition to her anti-family bias streak.

Anyway, she came up behind me at the counter and asked, "How did you like the exhibit?" And I said I had enjoyed myself and turned to the person getting my T-shirts, thinking I'd talk to Lynn again shortly.

But that turned out to be the last time I saw her. She simply disappeared. I got my things and went across the street to look for her at the bar, but she wasn't there. I returned to the exhibit hall and looked around. I could have let it go but kept looking. I really didn't like the fact that we didn't at least say goodbye.

Saying goodbye is a big thing for me. I find it important, something I need to do even with a person I will never see again, even an acquaintance of a few hours or minutes. I felt the loss of her companionship and again, after being with this new friend for five hours, I was alone on the streets of Memphis. And I had eight more hours to go until my train would leave for Chicago.

Mud Island

I decided I would walk through Mid-America Mall, and let the walk come up with some options. I could find a place for dinner, head back to the Peabody, listen to the night's live comedy, and then take a cab from there to Amtrak at about 11:30 p.m.

The mall was once again deserted. The federal and county government workers, the bankers, the lawyers, and the secretarial workers had all left. The afternoon was hot, and the sun was starting its final journey westward.

As I walked I remembered Mud Island. I headed in that direction. Lynn had told me about the Island. Some years before, the Mississippi deposited a large amount of mud just off downtown. After some thinking, and acceptance of the fact that the mud island would always be there, the city decided to make the island into a park. City officials built a jogging/physical fitness area, a Mississippi River Museum, and a replica of the southern 1,000 miles of the Mississippi and connected downtown and the island with a tram.

I walked the few blocks to the admissions gate and bought a $1.50 ticket for the tram ride. I declined a museum ticket, as I figured I'd seen enough exhibits with Ramses. I was still a bit lonesome after losing my companion but was willing to try this new experience. The tram ride is short, perhaps a minute and a half, but you do see the Memphis bridges and can see downtown from this perspective.

I got off the tram and walked down the several flights of stairs to the replica of the river. I was surprised by the work that had gone into this. Laid in concrete was a scale model of the southernmost 1,000 miles of the river to a scale of one foot per mile. The "river" was a flowing stream of water, depth, width, and floodplain presented to scale.

I walked to the beginning of the walking tour, where the various watersheds from northern states were depicted by slate walls with the names of states and rivers, over which came water that cascaded into the Ohio, Missouri, and other river systems, which then fed into the main body of the Mississippi.

As I walked along the flowage, I could see the various depths and widths of the river and would also see the various cities and towns that were built on the river's edge at certain points: St. Louis, Memphis, Vicksburg, New Orleans, all presented to scale, laid out as a metal surface complete with street layouts.

There were signs along the way with bits of information about various changes in the river and its plain over the years and how these changes affected certain towns and villages.

The afternoon sun was hot, and I enjoyed the warm air as I traveled along the Mississippi. There were a few other people around. I walked along to New Orleans and then to the Gulf of Mexico, a large pool of water with a sign: "No wading in the Gulf of Mexico."

I noticed a beverage cart and thought it smart of the entrepreneurs to place this at the end of the hot walk down river. There was a small restaurant nearby, with a patio area and umbrella tables. I noticed a rock band setting up near the patio. I decided to walk to the actual river, and as I approached I saw a large boat pushing six barges with the current toward one of the Memphis bridges.

The current was strong, the river was full of debris, and the barges were moving fast. As the barges approached the bridge, I noticed them slowing down so as to negotiate the river's bend and to glide between the pylons supporting the bridge. After watching this scene a while, I decided to return to the Gulf of Mexico and have a beer.

The Party

The drink carts were all set for business, and they were selling drink tickets at a ticket table, which you would redeem for refreshment. I bought a couple of beer tickets, got a beer, and then walked over to the patio area.

There weren't many people there, just two women holding tables for friends. I chose a table nearby.

I realized the sun was burning on the right side of my face, and that I selected the only table without an umbrella. I moved my chair back about three feet from the table, for a bit of shade from the nearby building.

As I sipped my beer, I watched the musicians in the band set up and listened to them tune their instruments. People started coming and filling the patio area. A radio station van drove near the band and began to set up antennae. A television truck came.

More people arrived. One woman's husband showed up, and the other woman's six female friends arrived. I had stumbled onto a major party! A waitress came by, and I ordered another beer. I wanted to see what was happening.

Two young women came by, saw my table, and asked if I were using that table. I said, "Not really, you can use it," as I was really not at the table, simply three feet away. The beer started to take effect, and I looked to my left and saw the beautiful Memphis skyline, shining in the 5:30 p.m. sunlight.

I got another beer. I began to realize that I would have to walk through that downtown sooner or later, and that I'd prefer to do it when it was light. I needed to find a place to eat, and then I'd return to the Peabody. I'd better stop the beers soon, I thought, if I wanted to be alert for my walk through downtown.

I also had another decision to make. Would I just get

up and leave, or could I engage the two women in some conversation and learn about life in Memphis. After several minutes of wondering, the band by now playing its loud music, I mustered the nerve to move into their sphere.

I'd have to move my chair, a definite physical commitment from which there would be no turning back. I tried to move the chair and speak at the same time, and scraped the metal on the concrete as I said, "Excuse me, would you mind if joined you for a few minutes?" I was already joining them so they really had no choice.

I introduced myself, and the dark haired woman to my right said she was Molly, and her friend was "Shay-la." I wanted to comment to Shayla about that interesting and unique name, but then realize her name was "Sheila," but in southern talk it's pronounced "Shayla."

Molly seemed the friendliest, and "Shayla," on my left and closer to me, seemed a bit unsure about all this. They were drinking wine coolers ("wan" – like "fan," as Molly pronounced it), and I realized I missed my chance to more deftly enter their sphere when I failed to buy them a refill the last time the cocktail waitress came by. I began to ask them questions, such as what this party was all about.

They told me this was sponsored by a radio station that went to various scenes around Memphis as a way to promote the sites. The station was helping promote the first of many "sunset parties" on Mud Island at Crawdaddie's Restaurant, on whose patio we sat (at the Gulf of Mexico on the river walk).

I mentioned I had come from Wisconsin to see the Ramses exhibit, and they were surprised someone would come from that far for that exhibit. They knew 100,000 people were coming in August to commemorate the 10th anniversary of Elvis' death, but were surprised that anyone would make a pilgrimage to see the Ramses exhibit.

I asked about good restaurants, and the women suggested a few.

At this point a young man walked up, a friend of Molly. He was introduced to me as Rick. He stood, because there were no more chairs, and I offered him my chair if he'd like. Declining, he said he'd like a beer, and the women were about finished with their coolers.

So Rick and I got up to get some drink tickets. It turned out Rick was born in Milwaukee and was a Brewer and Packer fan. We had something in common to talk about, and we returned with our drinks.

After some chatter back and forth, and watching the growing crowd – many different kinds of people: men with three-piece suits, women in summer white dresses, men in various kinds of baseball caps, women in punkish outfits – Molly and Rick talked and I asked Sheila what she did. She said she was a controller for a company and she was going to school to get an MBA.

We ordered more drinks and listened to the music. I began to feel that I had to either leave, if I wanted to negotiate my way to the Peabody safely, or make friends pretty fast. I told the group what I had planned, and that the more I drank with them, the more dependent I was on them to get me to the Peabody.

They had no problem with that, so we ordered another round. The sun was setting, the music was loud, the company nice, and the crowd interesting. I was having a great time with my new friends.

I asked them about Graceland. Rick told about bumper stickers that you can get that say, "I was asked to leave Graceland." He talked of the time he and a friend went to one of the three gift shops and laughed and laughed at all the atrocious Elvis plastic crap for sale. But the diehard fans who take this very seriously as a form of worship don't take that too kindly. Many "disrespectful" people have been asked to leave by the management. It is a mark of status among some Memphians to be asked to leave!

The three of these folks were all educated at Arkansas, "razorbacks." I gave Molly some heat about her accent: "It's not 'wan,' it's wiiine."

I suggested we all go to dinner, and they thought about where we should go. The party was beginning to break up — it was 8 o'clock by now and getting dark, and most were going on a riverboat ride. My friends debated a bit as to whether we should go on the ride, but Molly settled it all by saying, "There won't be a bar on the boat."

So we walked back to the tram to ride across to the parking lot where their three cars were to go to supper. They selected Charles Vergo's Rendezvous on South 2nd Street, where we could get ribs. My friends felt this was the best place to go for someone visiting Memphis for the first time. We got into Sheila's new Toyota and headed for the restaurant

The place reminded me of Larry Blake's Rathskeller in Berkeley: old wooden walls, old wooden tables and chairs, and clutter all over. The place was jammed with people, and the taped music was blues.

We ordered pork chops with sauce, which were recommended over the ribs, and our meals were served on paper plates with slaw and beans. There were two thick chops on each plate and plenty of sauce. A pitcher of beer, and we were set. Sheila told a story about her strangest date, which didn't end well when the guy got a little lewd.

I managed to talk about how wonderful this night was with them, how rare it is to find good friends on a chance encounter, and how I'd always remember this. We finished our excellent food, and the three of them headed for the bathrooms to relieve the drink-induced bladder pressure.

I went back to the open kitchen where all the black cooks were hard at work and complimented them on the fine food. We chatted back and forth, and I told them I'd tell everyone in Wisconsin theirs was the best food around. They thanked me profusely.

Rick came out and told me he and Molly had been going out here and there, which was why he had shown up tonight at the party. The gals appeared, and we headed for the Peabody for another drink. There we sat at the bar while the worst "comedy" any of us had ever heard went on a small stage to our left.

The bartender agreed with us that it was bad. He was a big black man, and I found out he had lived in Beloit, Wisconsin, for a while, and had been mugged at the Milwaukee Greyhound station. We couldn't believe that given his size, but he said he was a lot smaller then. He agreed with me that the name of the hotel should be pronounced "Pee-bdy" and my friends thought that strange.

Rick drew a caricature of me sitting at the bar, and

another of the bartender. It turned out both Rick and Molly were commercial artists.

We left the bar and headed for the car. It was by now 11:30 and time for me to get to Amtrak. As we drove the deserted street I had walked hours earlier, Sheila said she had never been down this way. We passed one lit place, a bar, with an older black woman who seemed to be dressed as a prostitute and an older man with her.

When we came to a stoplight and realized we had gone too far, we were going to do a U-turn when we spotted an unmarked police car. We lucked out that time by not making the turn. We legally turned around and headed back toward the Amtrak station.

As we drove into the parking area, both Sheila and Molly asked, "Are you sure we want us to leave you here?" They were quite shaken by the appearance of the neighborhood and train station. I said, "Yes, and thank you so much for a wonderful time."

I kissed Molly and Sheila, shook Rick's hand from the back seat, and bravely got out into the night, heading straight for the station.

Within a few minutes the train arrived, and we set out for Chicago at 12:05 a.m. Again I had two seats to myself. With a belly full of beer and chops and a heart full of the day's experiences and the people I had met, I easily fell asleep.

Journey's End

I awoke somewhere in Illinois, on a rainy and dreary morning. Across the aisle was a very young black woman, perhaps 17 years old, with her baby, a cute little boy of about nine months. I admired her for bringing him on the train, sleeping with him and comforting him when he wanted to cry. He loved to look out the window. When he'd see something, he would make noises and widen his eyes and jump up and down. I wondered what would become of him when he would be a teenaged boy living in a Chicago ghetto. I was sad to think that his fresh vitality might easily give way to the lethargy of drugs and the ruthlessness brought on by an expensive habit. Hopelessness out of a hopeful beginning.

We returned into Chicago by the same route we left, and I watched the deserted factories and blighted parking lots as we rode into downtown.

We arrived on schedule, and I was able to hustle to the Fox Lake commuter train in time. As we rode through the Illinois countryside I saw the new factories going up, now in the suburbs, and noticed that while their main buildings were designed well and looked more attractive than their counterparts in the city, the semitrailers and litter in the parking lots still looked the same. There seemed to be no progress, only an escape from the city, at the expense of blacks and minorities who now populate the city in a majority.

I arrived in Fox Lake in the rain, drove to Williams Bay, and completed my journey tired but feeling richer for the hours spent on the road – and in Memphis, Tennessee.

Thanks to Rick (wherever he is) for his lovely caricature of me, drawn on a napkin!

LESSONS FROM THE WEIGHT ROOM

"The Scene"

There are a lot of radio, television, and newspaper ads extolling the virtues of "working out" as a way to feel good about one's self by improving the look and shape of one's body. Thin, attractive women pose holding weights and wearing spandex and sweatbands. Young, smooth-chested men beam as they stand next to an attractive woman while subtly flexing biceps and pectorals. Vic Tanny, Cher, Victoria Principal, and Glenn Frey are some of the names associated with a growing business that seems to focus on 20 to 30-year-old yuppies who want to look good so they can attract beautiful people to themselves, all the while building power and success in their professional lives.

My Scene

I enjoy playing volleyball. Much of the competition I face in the church league is younger and more flexible. While pondering how to maintain myself as a good competitor, I reasoned that a workout program would keep my body flexible, and the added strength would result in a better spiking game.

Another possible motivation is turning 40 years old and recognizing at some level that if I ever want to improve my strength, now would be my opportunity. My own negative feelings about "the scene" were put on hold as I spoke with the fitness director at the local YMCA. He confirmed my goals and said he could put me on a program that would help me attain them.

Lessons

The Weight Room

The YMCA is not a Vic Tanny. The facilities are clean and attractive, looking more like high school facilities than a glass-and-leather corporate fitness center. The equipment is adequate, yet spartan. There is no glamour in pulleys, weight plates, and assorted devices designed to make you work. It becomes quite clear than any notions of "working out" and quickly attaining a new model-quality body are ad-agency fantasies.

The People

After nearly five months of thrice-weekly visits to the weight room, I have seen a lot of different people. "The scene" is actually more diverse than one would think, perhaps a result of the nature of the YMCA, a simple, affordable community facility, not a private club. I have seen all kinds of people from all walks of life: college football players, wrestlers, firefighters, police officers, real estate agents, laborers, city and hospital employees, homemakers, business executives, and retired folk.

There are young people in their late teens and twenties, and I have seen older people, even some in their seventies and eighties, in the weight room.

The bodies take all forms: extremely thin, average, perfectly muscled, wrinkled and elderly, overweight. I regularly see a 45-year-old man with one leg and a young man in his twenties with one arm and have seen a young woman in a wheelchair pumping iron. The outfits are pretty standard, usually sweatpants and sweatshirts, some shorts and T-shirts (my attire), and only several women in spandex. Two of these caught my attention to the point of distraction, as their outfits were tight and revealing from top to bottom. Most men and women dress modestly, and even the most muscular have never called attention to themselves.

Working Out

Having done this for some weeks, I appreciate knowing how the muscled bodies come from hard work, diet, and discipline. I went up to one guy who had a nice build and asked him how long he'd been working out. He told me fifteen years. No wonder he looked the way he did!

Every person in the room is concentrating and working. There is strain, there is fatigue, and there is conversation in between. Between sets of lifts, the person rests, and some huddle to talk about work, sports, and workout programs. Some come with a friend or friends and help one another do the best they can. A spirit of community begins to develop among familiar faces. In here is common sharing of equipment, and courtesies are extended: People negotiate use of equipment, ask each other for help, and offer encouragement.

As a newcomer, and a thin person, I have never experienced anyone judging me for my inexperience or the look of my body. There is mutual acceptance of one another's level of fitness, endurance, and strength. There is a feeling of camaraderie because all share the discipline, the work, and the desire for improvement.

The Inner World

Concentration is required for safety and for the best performance. Breathing and willpower, components of any meditation technique, are important to weight training. One fault I find with many of my compatriots is negative attitude. I once admired a young man from a distance, noting the intensity of his workout, the look of his upper body, and the impressive number of weights he could pull and lift. One day he and I were together in the locker room, and I made a comment about how well he seemed to be doing. He countered immediately by saying how upset he was that he wasn't doing better, that he just wasn't improving.

The attitude of "whatever I do is not good enough" seems to prevail with too many of my cohorts. Most every time I comment to people about their levels, they speak of how dissatisfied they are and how much further they have to go. In here are exceptions, and these people have a ready smile and a friendly attitude and seem quite comfortable with themselves.

A Personal Note

My body has changed after these weeks of working out. My legs and arms are stronger, and my chest and legs are more developed. My shirts are tighter in the neck, arms, and shoulders. I can see a difference in my arms and chest and can feel a difference in my arms. Initial feelings of aggressiveness have subsided, and I have since learned those are a result of too strenuous of a workout.

After each workout I feel accomplished, having first taken the time to get to the YMCA and, second, having run through my routine. There have been times when I have thought, "Why bother?" and times while on the machines that I have questioned what I was doing there. Each time, though, I feel good that I keep the discipline, that I accomplish the exercise, and that I devoted the time to it. Personal feelings of satisfaction, and the sense of well-being after exercise keep me feeling good immediately following the workout and in the rest days between.

And, by the way, my volleyball spike is much stronger, and I have noted certain strength and flexibility improvement!

WHAT WOULD JESUS DRIVE?

Some years ago someone came up with the phrase, "What Would Jesus Do?" and then we starting seeing jewelry and bumper stickers with the initials WWJD. One day I found myself behind a car with that bumper sticker, and it got me thinking about WWJD, "What Would Jesus Drive?"

A few days later, that question still in the back of my mind, I was at one of our mainline church seminaries where some in the faculty dining room were discussing whether Bonhoeffer's theology of violence was a poignant example of situational ethics or just a futile "too little, too late" act of desperation. This discussion was on the heels of another one about laughable "Catholic kitsch art" and how the postmodern condition is better described by modern European existentialists.

And just before walking out to the parking lot I was engaged with a professor who looked askance when I suggested that United States voters will never rid us of the military-industrial complex. Silly me for failing to believe voters might be ready for a radical pacifism that would then miraculously become U.S. military doctrine!

With all of these issues swimming in my pastoral mind I found myself in the seminary parking lot. Noticing the signs "Faculty and Staff Parking Only: All Others Will Be Towed Away," I couldn't help but notice what was parked in those precious spots nearest the seminary entrances: SUVs and other shiny, late-model cars, certainly costing as much to lease or own as a modest home in a small town. The devilish question came to mind, "WWJD?" or "What Would Jesus Drive?"

Ivan Illich once wrote about a North American

penchant for devoting vast quantities of resources to automobiles. He said the average American car owner spent many hours working to pay for the car, the insurance, the upkeep, and the gasoline and oil, and dividing the total cost by one's hourly wage, and then dividing the total annual mileage by that number, you see how many miles you get for each hour you work.

Illich figured that Americans got an average of five miles an hour, or five miles for every hour worked. That's what a peasant can walk, he wrote, and at far less damage to the environment.

What Would Jesus Drive is a good question? Or would he drive at all? What would his choice of vehicle be? To my relief I spotted What Jesus Would Drive in the last seminary faculty and staff parking slot: a beat-up, rusty, old Ford station wagon.

Last in a line of those fashionable mid-sized SUVs and sporty Volvos, this would certainly be what Jesus drove! I wondered if there was some bumper sticker, some symbol, some clue as to what this faculty member taught. Would it be New Testament studies? Prophetic literature in the Old Testament? The sociology of Ancient Israel? Feminism and re-imaging?

As I got closer the truth was revealed: The back of the old Ford was full of paint cans and dropcloths. At first I was disappointed that this wasn't the vehicle of some professor of itinerant New Testament radicalism or Latin American liberation theology. Of course, it could have been, but to my mind the car was owned by someone on the seminary's maintenance staff.

But then I felt better. Certainly that car was closer to something the carpenter of Nazareth would drive, a rusty,

44

old thing capable of hauling his gear and much more affordable than one of those gas-guzzling, polluting SUVs.

As so many look to Jesus to help with family values and radical analyses of post-modern society, maybe we should look for guidance on what to drive. Is it fair to look at what's sitting in our church parking lots and ask ourselves the relationship of what we drive to the *Shema*, or the Great Commission, or the second commandment?

Or maybe he walked or rode a bicycle instead, getting exercise, saving non-renewable resources, not polluting the creation's air, and having hundreds and thousands of dollars available to give to the world's poor instead of to the petroleum, automobile, and insurance industries of the world. That would be the truly radical thing to do.

ARNIE

Saturday night, September 29, 1984

Three-hour boat wedding, Geneva Lake

I met a friend tonight.

His name was Arnie.

Arnie is a teacher who teaches computer studies in
Evanston. Arnie is about 35, getting married November 11.
His fiancée is a social worker, on retreat in the northwoods.

Arnie believes in reincarnation.

He believes in genius in the ghettos of Chicago. He loves to
play blackjack.

Arnie has stayed at the MGM Grand in Reno. He has
visited the Mustang Ranch because a relative (woman) is
manager. We talked casino experiences.

We talked L.A./S.F.

We talked about after-death experiences.

Arnie talked fast. He also asked questions. We talked about
dealing with people and bearing their sorrow.

I could have stayed with him all night. But he got cold as
we sat in the cool winds off the lake.

And we didn't talk again.

I even forgot to seek him out to say goodbye. But then, he was gone before I could say goodbye.

We could have visited. I could have gone to his wedding. He could have met me here or halfway from anywhere.

But we left without saying goodbye.

I will never see Arnie again. I miss him like I don't miss anyone else. I have lost a friendship that almost developed. A miscarriage of a soul mate.

We enjoyed each other for those moments.

And that was it.

Except for the sense that time slips away. That the "ships in the night" still pass. That time and experience are to be enjoyed now, regardless of futures unknown.

Arnie had curly, bushy hair. An easy manner.

I enjoyed his company. Immensely. And I think now I have lost a future, a little future.

I miss Arnie, my friend.

SMOKY LINK

The day was sunny and warm, and the sky was cloudless, but something still seemed dark about it. Maybe it was the way the farmer's truck was parked next to the pen. The back was open and a splintery, sun-bleached old ramp angled down from the bed of the truck to the gate of the pen. The farmer was opening the gate to the pen, and the other pigs were beginning to sense something was strange about him this morning. They were grunting and squealing their surprise as they began to stand up on the sun-baked ground.

Suddenly the farmer yelled to the big sow to "get on up there" and next, in a quick motion, rapped me on the back with a long stick and shouted at me to get on up the ramp, too. As the old sow grunted on her way up, I knew why I felt darkness come over this beautiful day: When the others walked up this same ramp, they never came back. The word was they went somewhere at the end of the road, but no one seemed to know where or why. And now the time had come for me and the sow.

I tried to turn my head to look back to the dusty ground of our pen and to watch the others as they stirred along the edges of the fence. But the farmer kept yelling and poking, so I followed the old sow as she kept walking up into the truck. and I felt a sudden sadness come over me like one of those billowy dark clouds that sometimes drifted over the sun and shadowed the earth.

The inside of the truck was dark and hot, even though occasional lines of sun slid through the slits in the dirty wooden panels that formed the sides and roof of the back of the truck. There were strands of straw on the floor, and flies, clusters of flies, spinning this way and that in the confines of this new pen.

The farmer pushed the ramp up and over the truck's rear opening, blocking my view of the pen and the others as they were settling and scratching their bellies on the hard, dry ground or loping over to the narrowing but adequate strip of wet, cool mud in the center of the pen.

The sow stood off to the right, trying to stick her wet nose out of one of the broken corner sections of the truck's paneling. I felt a slight tilt to the left as the farmer got into the front of the truck, heard the slam of a door, and then a pitched grind and a rumble as the truck's motor started. Pops and muffled poots came out of the rear pipe, and the sow and I both lurched backwards as the truck began to move forward.

I could hear the whine of the transmission and the low gurgle of the gears as the truck picked up speed, billowing up dust as we surged forward along the road. The sow still stood in the corner, trying to stick her nose out into the blowing and warm air. I stood watching, waiting, and wondering.

Through a small crack in the floor I could see the gray-white of the gravel and then a blacker surface as the ride became smoother.

Something was not right about this, standing still while this truck was moving. There was no sky to see, only the rough, dried wood beneath me, and wheels and blurring road colors beneath that. Every so often I could hear a whoosh of something moving past us in the other direction, soundlessly, save for a sudden exchange of wind and air.

After a while, the truck's sound began to change, and the constant whine of the engine seemed to let up, until the gears ground together and the noises changed as our speed slowed. Were we coming to the end of the road?

The truck stopped and then suddenly lurched in the opposite direction, pushing the sow's nose into her corner and sending me toward the middle of the truck. The sow began to grunt and breathe more quickly. I could feel the hairs of my ears standing on end, and I began to breathe more quickly. too.

The farmer was slamming the door and getting out of the truck, and when he got to the back he was fooling with the pins holding the ramp in place. As he opened the ramp I eagerly turned to see what was at the end of the road. I noticed the old sow turning her head, too, as if to acknowledge that she had arrived somewhere she wasn't sure about it either.

As the ramp was lowered, I could see the farmer and another farmer with him. This one wore a white hat, the smooth, shiny kind worn by the farmers who crawled up tall poles over which were strung long, dark lines. He also had on a long white coat, and it was splattered with grease and mud – or was it redder than that?

"Git on down here," the farmer yelled, and the sow grunted and began to move forward, while I stood and watched. "Come ON. Get the hell down here!" he shouted and began to wave his stick. As I moved from the back of the truck I could see out of the corner of my eye that to the left was a river, flowing next to the building, and off to my right was a larger building. I could see that at the bottom of the ramp was a narrow passage fenced in on both sides, and next to that I could see small pens, with one or two other pigs in each one. Was this what was at the end of the road – another pen?

But the ground was not hard-packed dirt and dust, nor was there any mud hole: It was hard and gray, but solid as rock, and smooth. This floor was bare, save for a few droppings and the ever-present specks of flitting flies circling and diving and spiraling in their crazy patterns.

After walking off the truck, the farmer and the man with the hat led the sow to the pen to the right and me to one on the left. There was another younger pig in my pen, and he stood with his nose poking through a space between two of the railings. The farmer walked back toward the truck, and the man with the hat walked into a door that led into a dark room.

All at once the dull summer air was broken with a screaming and squealing I had never, ever heard before. I frantically looked around as my pen mate froze and then pulled his head through the railing and jumped backward.

The piercing noise came from the dark room, pulsing out in wave upon wave of tortured sound. The commotion was deafening as the screams bounced off the walls of that dark room, back and forth, up and down, until the voice began to fade, and the cries got shorter, and then with one high pitched wail, the screams stopped, and all was quiet again.

I could hear the sound of a farmer's radio, with the voice coming out of the box and the happy music rolling over the dark room's summery air. Then there was a splash, a single, loud splash like water pouring into a trough. Then the farmer with the white hat came to the pen across the way, opened the door, and pushed the old sow out with a slap on her hind quarters. She gave out an unhappy grunt, showing not bewilderment but just a hint that her afternoon was being interrupted by this farmer and he had better have a good reason.

Just then I could hear a whooshing sound like something I heard once when the farmer was repairing some metal railings while holding fire in his hand. I could smell something like the time the cow was struck with lightning near our pen, a hot, pungent smell, when hair and fire meet.

As my thoughts floated back to that terrible day, when the floating cloud erupted into a white-blue flash and streaked down in a crackling sort of upside-down tree with branches going this way and that, heading straight for the cow as she bellowed in fear and then was struck as her eyes bulged out of her head and her tongue shot outward, and the smell, the smell as her legs slowly, ever so slowly, buckled beneath her, and her tail stood straight out and then the . . . . But just then the sow's scream pierced through my memory.

My eyes opened wide as I heard that calm old sow from my pen cry out in wave after wave of horrific screeching. What unspeakable things was that farmer doing to her in that dark room?

Between the screams I could hear that voice from the box, talking about someone's market with fresh meat and eggs, now blending with the screams so that I became dizzy and began to feel frantic. My pen mate and I both began to shift nervously on our feet, and we swayed back and forth to the regular, pulsating rhythm of the sow's screams of fear and distress.

She yelled in surprise and in terror, and it sounded like she was pleading in the hope that whatever it was would stop. Her cries became shorter and weaker. I could hear the voice in the box and what sounded like a bucket full of water falling onto the cold, hard floor, and then she stopped screaming altogether.

From the dark room after the sound of the splash came the whooshing sound, and then the smell, and I remembered the cow and the lightning. Just then the farmer came and pushed my pen mate out the gate and onto the walkway and into the dark room, the scream room.

Across the way was one more pig, and she looked at me with eyes that seemed to ask, "have you ever heard such things before?" I began to shift back and forth, almost swaying to the music that came from the voice box, now knowing why no one back at my pen with the mud in the center could explain what was at the end of the road.

There was no way to really make sense out of it, and no one could ever imagine what went on here, even those who saw the cow struck with the blue fire.

I startled as the screams began again, and I knew my pen mate was seeing what the old sow had seen moments earlier. I looked at the pig across the way as I began to feel dizzy with fear. As I stood, swaying, with flies swirling at my back, I heard the familiar rhythm of sound bursting from the dark room, first the screams, then the splash, then the whoosh, followed by the smell.

My head instantly cleared as I realized the farmer with

the white hat was walking towards my pen now, stick in hand. He opened the bolt on the metal gate and said, "Your turn, Smoky Link," as he slapped my rear with the stick and pushed me toward the room of darkness.

When I looked into that room I could see why my friends had screamed, but what kept me from screaming I don't know. Just ahead were three motionless hogs, hanging upside down from a railing suspended from the ceiling. Their hind feet were stretched apart and hanging by the tendons from wooden dowels attached to steel hooks dropped from a pulley which rode on a suspended rail. Each hog was split down the middle of its body, from the rear end all the way to just beneath the head.

The old sow was motionless – and at peace. There were two other farmers in the dark room, one hunched over the form of my pen mate on a table and the other standing by the voice box with a knife in his hand. The farmer who came to get me from the pen pushed me farther into the dark room, and I became fully alert.

But before I knew what had happened, he grabbed one of those metal hooks and slid it between my hind leg and my tendon and with his other hand pushed a button on a handle of some kind. I realized I was being pulled, upside down, toward the railing just below the ceiling.

I began to scream, like the others, out of sheer fright. I kicked my free leg and yelled and yelled, and I thought I saw the lone hog in the pen just outside the dark room as I swung from side to side, upside down. I saw a ray of sunlight come streaming in through a window and then saw the bright, sharp blade in the hand of the farmer standing just below me.

I felt a sharp ripping pain as he poked that blade into my neck. and I screamed out in horror as I felt the warmth of something running under my head and dripping off my chin to the floor below. I kicked and I screamed and knew I couldn't stay like this very long. My mind, crazed with fear, remembered that singed cow, and I thought this was even worse. The cow didn't know what happened to her, but I am feeling this and screaming and kicking and seeing my friends motionless just a few feet away.

I kicked and kicked and could feel that hook in my tendon and could feel myself swinging back and forth on that railing. How could the farmer do this to me? With every ounce of strength, every bit of rage I could muster, I kicked harder and harder, and with one great squeal of disbelief and hope and despair I shuddered and kicked with all the energy I had left in my body.

With a start I felt my tendon rip off the hook and I crashed to the hard, cold floor. I landed on my back, just off to the side of my neck, and for an instant lay there, feeling as surprised as the farmer standing next to me looked. In a flash I was scrambling to my feet, almost getting tangled in my four legs as they started to work simultaneously.

I ran to the doorway that led to the light and passed the pen with the lone pig staring at me with her mouth open and her eyes bugging out as if she had been struck by lightning, and I reached the end of the wooden slatted boardwalk and to my surprise hit ground that felt familiar with dust and small stones underfoot and patches of green grass.

Immediately ahead was a large building, in front of

which was a large flat area full of cars, some moving, others parked. It looked like farmers and farm children were walking among the cars, going in and coming out of the building. A large sign on the side of the building said, "Fresh Meats and Produce."

I couldn't run into all those farmers and their cars, and I couldn't run to the left, with the other building and its cars and trucks. I instinctively ran to the right, aware that behind me the farmers were running from the dark room and shouting, "Hey, come back here you stupid pig!"

To the right was the dark brown river I had seen as I left the truck to walk down the ramp towards the dark room. I hesitated a moment, but with the yelling farmers behind me, I leaped into that water. I sank below the surface, and it felt cold and dark like the mud hole of my pen. The burning in my throat cooled down, and even the hole that was pushed open by that shining blade felt like it was closing up.

My head surfaced, and my eyes bulged with fear as I blew air and water out of my snout and as my four legs with their cloven hooves cut and flailed at the brown water. For the first time since I had left my pen at the end of the road I had always known, I was once again aware of the bright sunshine.

It was the kind of day that was perfect for lying against the edge of the railing, soaking up the warmth of the light until my hide began to feel like it was ablaze with the sun, then slowly getting up and walking over to the mud hole and slowly sinking into its thick, enveloping peacefulness.

The cold water covered my head for a few moments, reminding me I had better keep slashing at that water with my hooves – there is no peace in this enveloping brown liquid. As I blew the water out of my nostrils I once again remembered the horror of the dark room, the three still bodies hanging upside down from those hooks on the railing, and I felt a shot of another surge of energy though my system. Somehow I managed to get to the middle of the lazy, brown river.

I began to struggle, moving first to the left, and then to the right, until I noticed what looked like dusty and familiar ground ahead, giving me a direction once again.

A dizziness began to come over me, reminding me of when I heard the sow and then my pen mate screaming and squealing their lives away. A sudden weakness began to overtake me, and my legs slowed their choppy motion. Just ahead was dusty, dry ground and the sun was shining brightly. Oh, if I could only get there, I could rest, I could lie in the sun, I could awaken and be back in my old pen.

I was getting closer. The edge of the river was just ahead. There was mud, and there were large smooth stones. Green grass seemed to cover the ground above the bank. My hooves chopped at the water and then – could it be – mud, thick, gooey, mucky mud, but I must keep going. My legs carried me through that cool mud, and I landed on that shoreline and lifted and staggered my feet to the bank of the river with its patches of green grass and hard, dusty soil.

A building loomed ahead, off to the right. I didn't see any cars, and, oh, was that a pen ahead, with, yes, with a railing shining in the sunshine? In the center of the pen was a mud hole. It couldn't be, but it was true!

I walked next to the building and I felt very dizzy, very woozy, and so tired. I felt like I could sleep forever in that sunshine, and then I was ever so slightly aware that something – maybe water? maybe mud? – was dripping from my neck onto my chest and off my chest onto the ground.

The sunshine feels so good, and I am at peace, here in the bright light. I lay down, and I close my eyes. I am hardly breathing, but I don't need to breathe to feel this peace. What did that sign say on the building, "Bob and Mary's PABST Tavern"?

Off in the distance a truck approached, with its engine racing, and farmers with white hats were in that truck. But that didn't matter to the pig they called "Smoky Link," for he was in a cloud of cool mud where they would never find him. Neither would they be able to hang him from the suspended railing, ever again.

Author's note: The idea for the story is based on true events at a Wisconsin slaughterhouse where a pig kicked free from his hook, ran out of the building, jumped in the river, swam across, and died next to a tavern. My coworkers at the meat plant told me the story. Other details in the story are based on my experience working one afternoon on the hog line at the slaughterhouse on a day when they were desperate for help. Because the bosses sensed my squeamishness, my only job was to use a blowtorch to singe any hair left on the carcasses that had been freshly scalded in hot water.

Just a week ago, in July 2017, dozens of pigs got loose when the truck they were in overturned. Some were on the loose for a few days. Ironically, they were being taken to the "processing plant" that bought the company where I had once worked.

THE SPIRIT OF GENEVA LAKE

"All Is Calm," courtesy of Fred Noer

One Sunday during a sparkling Geneva Lake Memorial Day weekend, I joined a wedding party on board a Gage Marine cruise boat. Leaving the Riviera docks in Lake Geneva, we headed for a leeward shore just beyond Geneva Bay. As the captain slowed the engines, and the solemn pronouncement of marriage began, I suddenly noticed that we were surrounded by what seemed to be a three-ring circus.

High-powered speedboats roared by as seaworthy cruisers rumbled past, sailboats swept by, anglers bobbed atop the waves, scuba divers slipped into the cold and clear waters, and water-skiers skimmed past. Just as the newlyweds kissed, a skier waved as he soared by attached to a colorful hang glider. (We were also "mooned" by someone on a speedboat that had pulled up near to our boat!)

It was a typical Geneva Lake summer weekend, with people and boats plying the waters in all directions, blue skies above, crystal clear waters beneath, and lush green shores to the sides.

Winter enthusiasts enjoy a similar range of activities on the frozen waters of the lake. I remember a mild Sunday afternoon in January when the temperature hit 40 degrees, and the ice was as smooth and clean as plate glass. The sun was warm, the sky clear, the breezes gentle, and the lake frozen to a depth of 12 inches.

On that perfect winter's day, the Williams Bay ice was a giant ring of activity. Iceboaters sped to and fro, sails tight against the breeze. Large groups of anglers basked in the sun while chatting and watching their tip-ups. Ice skaters glided happily by while a pack of snowmobiles raced nearby. Four-wheel-drive trucks and four-door sedans cruised along the thick ice, heading nowhere in particular.

Families strolled across the ice with children sliding, dogs running, and sleds dragging behind. A lone motorcyclist roared past, studded tires barely gripping the smooth surface of the ice. When an airplane suddenly appeared out of nowhere and landed on the bay, I knew it was time to find a quieter place to enjoy the day.

For many, the spirit of Geneva Lake is typified by the

busy and often frenetic weekend activities of the different seasons. Others know how the lake has a life of its own, apart from our motors and wakes, our shouts and our laughter. For those persons, the spirit of Geneva Lake is best felt in those rare moments when the humans and their machines are absent from the lake.

Over the years I have been able to witness the lake's "hidden" spirit in those quiet moments when either the weather or the time of day allowed the lake to present other dimensions to its life.

I have skied across the lake and back during a driving noontime snowstorm, the only human foolish enough to be out on that frozen day. But the silence of the moment, as the snow deepened upon the ice, and as the shore became a whitening blur against the gray sky, called forth an eternally pristine essence. The lake was revealing itself to me in new ways because I allowed myself to stop and watch its silent beauty unfurl before me.

Once while skating across the smooth and mirrored ice in a full moon's midnight hour, I heard the cries of a lone screech owl along the silvered shore. I listened to the ice call back with great booms and cracks, as if to sing its own song of identity. The lake environment reclaimed its natural peace while people and machines slept in warm houses and garages.

On a quiet August night drifting in a silent sailboat, I felt the warm breezes against my skin, listened to the gentle lapping of the waves against the boat, and watched the light-years flash as meteorites streaked across the starlit sky. The heavens accented the lake's timeless beauty, highlighting eternity with this silent display of movement and light.

Hemingway wrote that Paris was "a moveable feast," an experience that would live with him all his days. The spirit of Geneva Lake is a "moveable feast" for all who linger by its waters for refreshment, and who later, in the midst of a busy day, summon its renewal during some daydreaming moment.

The lake is a living environment with a life of its own. It welcomes our happy and noisy forays unto its waters, and just as certainly invites us to feel its essence as we share solitary moments of quiet.

OWL, ICE, AND I

In the full moon's midnight hour

A lone screech owl voices its cry

Above the smooth and mirrored ice.

The silvered silent surface shifts

Its hidden mass in muffled booms,

Punctuating the night with its song.

Skate blades flash in the moonlight,

Cutting a rhythmic lane:

Owl, Ice, and I, a harmonic trinity.

LA BELLE CEMETERY

Photograph by the author

It's been twenty-five years since Grandpa and Grandma brought me to the old cemetery that was stretched along the shore of Fowler Lake, a placid Wisconsin lake. We had been fishing in Oconomowoc when Grandma decided she wanted to see the graves of her parents again. Toward the end of the afternoon we drove to the cemetery, and while Grandpa strolled along the gravestones, Grandma showed me the place where her parents were buried.

All these years later, I remembered only that they were at the edge of one of the narrow roads that ran through the cemetery and that the lake was nearby. On this particular October afternoon I had an hour until I was to meet friends for dinner, so I thought I'd go into the cemetery and look for my great-grandparents' graves. The wrought-iron gate was open, and I drove over the little bridge that spanned one of the lake's fingers and separated a short residential street from the cemetery.

This quiet city of the dead was alive with nature's gentle sounds: The breezes whispered through pine boughs and rustled oak leaves, chipmunks scampered over fallen leaves, birds sang, crows cawed, crickets chirped, and ducks quacked. I walked along the waterfront graves looking for the Hallett name.

I was certain the graves were somewhere near the water, and I quietly strolled by the scores of granite stones marking the final resting places of generations of local residents.

I walked the entire length of the waterfront and continued around the final circular section of graves. Atop this short hill of graves were two dozen metal markers clustered in a little group and silently speaking the names of infants who had died at birth or shortly thereafter.

As I circled around back toward the lake, I knew if I wanted to locate my family's graves I'd have to either backtrack the way I'd come or investigate an area farther from the shore. I told myself some quiet instinct would show me the way, and I thought I might close my eyes and turn myself around a couple of times, wait, and then allow my inner compass to lead me in the correct direction. Just as I thought I'd try this "scientific method" for finding these graves, I opened my eyes, looked down, and there they were, right in front of me! I'd stopped right in front of their graves.

A little more than a foot across, seven inches wide, and seven inches above the ground, the stones stated a simple message:

G. H. Hallet   M. R. Hallet

1870-1920   1871-1923

Just as I remembered, they were right next to the road, and off to the left was the lake. I stood in silent wonder as I beheld the graves of the great-grandparents I had never met. A lot had happened since I had been there so many years before. I began to speak towards the grave of George Henry Hallett:

"I'm glad to be here. I am your great-grandson, and we've never met. But your daughter, my grandmother, Florence, told me a lot about you. She told me how you, George, chauffeured for the Simmons family of St. Louis and how you were given the honor of driving the Presidential car when President Taft visited the Simmons family and the people of St. Louis. You didn't know that Florence had a son and named him after you."

To Minnie Rachel Hallett's grave I said, "Minnie, Florence told me how delighted you were to meet Jake when he was courting her and how you so appreciated the gifts of ice cream he brought for you. You didn't live to see them married in June of 1924. Their son George married and had four children, and I am Florence's first grandchild and the only one to know where you are buried."

"Over the years your two daughters remained very close to each other, even though May moved to California and lived there most of her life. As the one grandchild who also lived in California, I came to know May quite well, and she told me many stories of life as a chauffeur's child among the "rich people's children" in your old St. Louis neighborhood.

"I carried each of your daughters to their graves, and I said words of committal at their gravesites. I saw them to the end of their days. and you'd be pleased to know they each lived into their 80s, gaining a full thirty more years of life than each of you had."

As I looked at the graves, I noticed that someone looking at the stones would not know a thing about the lives of those buried beneath. Without a first name one would not know whether they were brothers, sisters, or husband and wife. I felt an important obligation to keep their memory alive and to communicate this place to my children so they too could become caretakers of the memories of the previous generations of our family.

The sounds came back to me as I continued to stand before the grave. As the trees, leaves, birds, animals, grasses, and insects made their presence known, the unexpected horn of a train broke my enchanted spell. How fitting, I thought, as I heard the engine thundering by and then the cars clacking over the tracks.

George and Minnie first arrived here by train when they accompanied the Simmons family on its summer trips to this area.

As the train quickly disappeared in the distance, and as the shadows of the late autumn afternoon began to settle upon the gravestones, I felt a mystical union with the past and the present in the living city of the dead.

Author's note: While George and Minnie spelled their name "Hallett," their gravestones inexplicably are misspelled as "Hallet."

Ghost Whistle

(A poem inspired by the visit to La Belle Cemetery)

The lonesome train whistle hung heavy in air

Sounding a full circle of time

Was it the train that first brought you both here,

In 19 hundred and 9?

I walked the old graveyard

Looking for them

Amid the green hills and oak.

I strolled the lakeshore

With crickets and ducks

Reading the names on the stone.

Grandma showed me where her parents lay

Some 25 years ago

Today I'm going to find them again

My instinct to show me the way.

Just then I looked down and right there they were laid

In 1920 and '23,

So I mustered my thoughts

And cleared out my throat

And this is what I said:

"I am your great-grandson

Whom you never met.

Your daughter told me of you

And the pride you took in your work, she said

How with horses you were the best.

But with cars better yet,

You drove for the rich,

Brought the doctor to the poor,

And once drove the president.

She named her one son in honor of you

A thing that you never knew;

And Minnie, I said, you loved ice cream I'm told

And that was the way to your heart.

You blessed your daughter to her beau, the one who

brought you ice cream, your sweet smile the camera caught,

A proud mother your 52 years.

I want you to know that your two girls stayed close

And each one had her own son . . .

They each lived to their 80s, adding 30 years more than

You had.

If it's any comfort, I said,

I carried your daughters to their graves

And over their tired old bodies said prayers

And sent them to you again."

The lonesome train whistle hung heavy in the air

Sounding a full circle of time

Was it the train that first brought you both here,

In 19 hundred and 9.

WHEN A FAMILY PET DIES

Every pet owner has to face the death of a pet. Like losing a trusted friend, the loss of a pet can be a terribly sad experience. With children, the death of a pet often presents their first encounter with death. They are sad because of their attachment to the pet, and they are curious because of their inexperience with death.

Helping children through the death of a pet can be a very rewarding experience for both the child and the adult. When we help children through the sad time, we teach them about the mystery of life and death, how to be thankful for the life the pet shared with them, and how to approach future experiences of having to face the death of some of the people they love.

The story below is about the death of a pet that had grown very old. The suggestions for helping children (and ourselves) through the death experience can be helpful in time of sudden death as well.

Our Family's Experience

Some years ago our first family cat died. At 15½ years, Clover was arthritic, prone to seizures, losing weight because of a possible tumor, and probably diabetic. We knew that we would have to "put her to sleep" one day, but the decision was hard because she was still able to function pretty well and because my wife and I had her since our marriage engagement. It was also hard to consider the cat's death since we knew it would be difficult for our young daughters, ages 6 and 9, who had known the cat all their lives.

After weeks of discussions and comments to the children such as "Clover is getting very old, and we will have to take her to the vet someday," we finally decided to set a date with the vet.

My wife called the vet and made arrangements for the vet to come to the house one morning while the children were in school. We would then keep the cat's body in a box until the children returned, break the news, and then bury her.

For three nights I said my goodbyes to Clover. She was curled under the writing desk in the living room at midnight the night before the appointment, and as I looked into her eyes and said my farewell, she gently curved her tail towards her eyes and covered them. I guess she didn't want to look at me at that hour.

Later, I watched as she drank from her bowl, noisily lapping the water into her mouth. Her body was in relief against the dim kitchen light, and I could see the jagged edges of her fur sticking up, a continual reminder of her unhealthy condition.

As I looked at her skinny body arched over the water bowl I remembered the time she was so fat that one night someone mistook her for a roaming raccoon. I thought, sometimes, that she looked like a large sausage.

There were days when she roamed our yard freely, stalking mice and large flies, munching on chipmunks, or prancing as a proud huntress with a squeaking young rabbit held by her sharp cat's teeth at the mane of its neck.

Sired by an orange-and-white father and a black mother, her brownish-orange coat always attracted the attention of our visitors. The Siamese in her prompted a high and conversant "meow" that responded to any attention.

Before her arthritis, she affectionately settled into any friendly lap. She loved to cuddle with the girls while they watched television or read, and they would gently stroke her soft fur.

On summer nights she'd lie in a bedroom's open window, nestled against the screen and soothed by the crickets' lullabies. She'd often curl on the bed next to the girls' pillows and breathe her gentle rhythm and emit her sweet and clean furry scent.

I awoke in the morning with a headache. I don't often get headaches, but when I do, I know they are attributable to some stress in my life. I knew that this headache was related to the planned visit from the vet and the fact that Clover would die.

After the girls went off to school, I said goodbye to Clover and stroked her behind her ears.

As soon as the vet came, we wrote out our check. We didn't want to have to do it later. The cat came in for some food and water, and the vet picked her up and wrapped her in a towel.

The first injection was the tranquilizer, and after hissing and showing great discomfort and disgust at having been medicated, she began to get comfortable, and lay down on the towel. The second injection worked its lethal dose within seconds, and being an old cat, Clover's heart stopped in about fifteen seconds.

When the vet left, we placed a towel in a small box and gently lowered Clover's furry body into it. By then both of us had splitting tension headaches. We sat on the couch, crying. We reminisced and laughed together about some of Clover's antics, and then I went to work. My headache was still there, and I decided I had it because I dreaded the

74

children's reactions later that day.

Later that afternoon, when both children were home, we sat them down and broke the news. Expecting hysteria, I was surprised by their composure. They had expected the news, they said, and were glad it was over with, because they had been dreading this final day. After more parental tears, we decided to go to the garage and see the body. I thought, "Someday when they do this in a funeral home, it might be easier for this experience."

We asked if the girls wanted to touch the cat's body, but neither of the girls wished to do so. They did look at her, and when I asked if they wanted to put anything in the box with her, they found two pieces of blue yarn and gently laid them on her fur. They remembered how Clover loved to play with strings and balls of yarn.

We took shovels to the backyard and, after looking at four possible gravesites, selected the right spot. We took turns digging, and then the girls went to the garage to bring the box containing Clover's remains.

I remembered the times I carried various relatives to their graves and cried in the gentle beauty of two young girls carrying a beloved pet to its grave, participants in the normal and inevitable cycles of living and dying, burying and remembering.

We turned the towel covering the cat and looked at Clover one last time, my wife and I bending down to stroke that soft, thick fur once more. The girls each began to cry, comprehending the magnitude of what was happening. We snuggled and caressed as the tears fell.

Each daughter was able to mention something humorous about what was happening, such as, "I'm glad this isn't one of us." As we lifted the box to gently lower it in the grave, a line of geese honked overhead. "A twenty-one goose salute," I suggested, marveling at the beauty of nature's timing.

We each grabbed a shovel and starting burying the box, taking time out to jump on the wet earth to tamp it down. Three rocks were placed upon the grave to mark the spot, and our oldest daughter added some dried corn as decoration. Later she would say, "This is the first time anyone really close to me has died."

At bedtime our youngest began to reminisce about Clover and then began to weep and weep. I had heard this six-year-old cry many times, but this time was different.

This was not the kind of crying associated with a skinned knee or hurt feelings; no, these tears sounded more like she had passed a threshold into a new world where death separates us from our loved ones. These tears were washing away infantile innocence, and she was growing into the world as it is, full of living and dying, joy and mystery.

Clover was dead, and her presence was already missed. Our family faced this experience together, each step taken in its own time. Our bonds were strengthened as we talked, grieved, viewed, made decisions, and buried our cat. We shared our feelings, faced death's mystery head on, and are buoyed into the present by sweet memory.

There are times when we expect to see the cat around the house. We can almost hear her meow and feel her presence. We are not rushing to get another pet to replace Clover, for she will never be replaced. But one day we will get another pet and probably have to go through the experience of life and death once again.

Suggestions For Handling
Your Pet's Death As A Family

As you read through my account of our cat's death, you may have noticed some of the ways we helped our children learn how to handle death.

1. Prepare your children in advance. Learn how to talk about death as a natural part of life. Anticipate that your pet will die someday, and talk gently about how each one of you would feel. What will you miss when your pet dies?

2. If you must end your pet's life because of infirmity or age, do not involve your children in the decision. This is an adult decision, and your children will not have to feel any guilt associated with a choice of such magnitude.

3. Take pictures of your pet so you will have plenty of reminders of its life. Be sure to look at those pictures as a family after the pet's death to remember some of the good times you had together.

4. Once you have decided that the time has come to see the vet, plan the whole experience step by step. Plan the date, the time, who will go to the vet's office, when the children will be informed, and what you will do together to grieve the pet's death. There is great sadness at this time, and it is better to express your feelings and get them all out. This is good practice for the time when you must face the death of a relative or close family member!

5. Decide how you will tell the children, and then sit together to allow feelings to be expressed and stories shared. There are sadness and humor. Be sure to ask, after the initial tears, "What do you remember best about _____?"

6. If you have decided to dispose of the body (many people choose to leave that to the vet or the humane society), try to have a viewing so the children know the reality of the death. This may seem difficult to do but is the best thing you can provide your children. They require many opportunities to deal with death directly.

7. If you are able to bury your pet in a suitable site (check your local ordinances on that), do it together. Dig the hole together. Carry your pet's "coffin" and lower it into the grave. Put in a flower or a memento. Say some words over the grave such as "We'll miss you," or if you're religious give thanks for the joy you had together. Tell some stories. Then together put the earth over the body and seal the grave. Put a marker on the grave if you like, or remember the spot for future visits.

To Summarize

As you join in these many activities together as a family you accomplish several important tasks:

– sharing feelings at a very emotional time and learning that it's OK to have the feelings and to express them.

– learning how to say goodbye to a beloved pet.

– learning how to say goodbye to a beloved person who will die one day.

– building stronger bonds as a family while going through these deep experiences together.

When a beloved pet dies, we experience a deeply sad time in our lives. By carefully living through the death and making sure that all family members are involved as much as possible in the goodbye process, we both honor our pet's memory and learn how to handle crisis as a family, becoming stronger and healthier people.

About The Author

Since having his first story about his grandfather published as a 19-year-old college student, Michael Bausch has gone on to write and edit newspaper articles, academic papers, original songs, books, sermons, college curricula, online university and graduate school courses, and blogs as well as produce multimedia digital media art with film, music, and art. To learn more about his work as a musician, author, pastor, digital media artist, and professor, visit his web page at michaelgbausch.com.

About The Publisher

Image Source, which is owned and operated by Fred Noer, provides writing and editing services and black-and-white photographic images of landscapes. For more information, go to the website www.frednoer.com.

www.ingramcontent.com/pod-product-compliance
Lightning Source LLC
Chambersburg PA
CBHW050555280326
41933CB00011B/1856